INTO MY VEINS

INTO MY VEINS

How to peel a peach with a cutthroat razor

Richard Levesley

authorHOUSE®

AuthorHouse™
1663 Liberty Drive
Bloomington, IN 47403
www.authorhouse.com
Phone: 1-800-839-8640

© 2011 by Richard Levesley. All rights reserved.

No part of this book may be reproduced, stored in a retrieval system, or transmitted by any means without the written permission of the author.

First published by AuthorHouse   10/25/2011

ISBN: 978-1-4670-0766-5 (sc)
ISBN: 978-1-4670-0767-2 (hc)
ISBN: 978-1-4670-0768-9 (ebk)

Printed in the United States of America

Any people depicted in stock imagery provided by Thinkstock are models, and such images are being used for illustrative purposes only.
Certain stock imagery © Thinkstock.

This book is printed on acid-free paper.

Because of the dynamic nature of the Internet, any web addresses or links contained in this book may have changed since publication and may no longer be valid. The views expressed in this work are solely those of the author and do not necessarily reflect the views of the publisher, and the publisher hereby disclaims any responsibility for them.

"This is how it all started"

I awoke to the sound of my own screams and a bead of sweat like a red hot stream of lava poured down the side of my face. Then it hit me, what I had done. At the age of eight I broke into my friend's house and stole his fireworks and I knew at that early age which way my life might turn.

Several years later in a smoke filled room, a heavy Jamaican bass playing, a black guy with a gold ring on each finger passed me a spliff. I took several draws and then everything became intense. I felt the beat of the music run through my body. I am fluent and over six feet tall and extremely handsome. I took a short taxi ride with Ringo Starr and I jumped out at the traffic lights, he was a cool guy. I found myself in Waldour Street. I heard Sam Cook sounds coming from a club called 'Flamingo.' I had to get in so I took off my jacket and hid it. This person came walking by and I said: "excuse me but I have just had my jacket stolen and I am desperate to get home." Without question 1 shilling was put into my hot, sticky hand.

In the club was the smell of a mixture of ganga and sweat. It was dark and alluring and in the centre was an organ playing some sweet rhythm and blues. It didn't take long before I was talking to Georgie Fame. We had a lot in common about the blues and girls. In the corner of the club was my destiny.

Two skinny men, smartly dressed, came up to me and said: "Want a jack?"

(A jack is a grain of heroin)

"How much?" I replied intuitively, not knowing what it was.

"One and six," said one of the men in a Greek accent.

"Two," I said sharply. I had already 'dipped' a handbag with well over £5. How to take them I thought to myself, better quit the Flamingo while I was ahead!

On the way out I was almost knocked over by a stocky, well-built bloke. He was wearing a pin striped suit and an expensive, paisley pair of shoes and the most distinguished feature was his mouth. It was heavily scarred. One of his entourage was driving a Rolls Royce, which stopped at a set of traffic lights. He was ambushed by a single punch to the mouth with a fistful of razors as he always had his window open (as I was to find out later). He was a notorious villain by the name of David Littvinof.

I took a stroll in the rain and when I heard some bluesy sounds that is where my destiny became a reality.

I took my two tabs and crushed them together and used a straw that I took from an empty coke bottle. I took one almighty sniff and I began to feel warm. It escalated into a roller coaster, wave after wave of euphoria. Several hours later in the 'Discothèque' I was feeling kinda sick so I went into the cloakroom and

Marc Bolan suggested a drink of coffee. He was working there at that time, good looking bastard! Phew, talk about destinies but I won't get into that just yet. I had no place to call home, so in the dirty filthy basement of the Establishment Club, I was physically exhausted and I crashed.

Robert Fraser (left), David Littvinof (Center) and Mark Bolan (right)

I was still tingling when I woke; where am I and what to do next?

I went back to the Discothèque to find the guys who sold me the "feel good" tabs. Upstairs is a gambling room, I put my last £1 on black and watched the roulette spin. The ball bounced perilously from the black slot and dropped into red. Marc told me an easy way to get some money. This is the road I mentioned earlier! Prostitution. My first experience was held in a house in Lyle Street. The punters paid their entrance fee, then they were allowed to watch a pornographic film and a live show. It was my turn. Two women, partially undressed and myself naked, put on a sexual act of various positions. Each time I did something different I had moans of gratification. I received a grand total of £5 and a dose of gonorrhea which was extremely painful when I took a piss! I went to the local VD clinic not knowing what I had but after several penicillin injections I soon found out what it was and never caught it again or any other diseases (thanks girls!) So off I went with my hard earned cash to get some smack.

It was quite difficult to find any smack. I had heard of a place where I might get some, it was in a bohemian cafe. I had no idea of how or what to expect. I soon got into what and how it was all about. So, (here we go) I was like an apprentice with a first year course, condensed into a one hit course. I didn't have any gear so, I took out from my hip pocket a hand full of cash and like a swarm of vultures they all wanted the same thing, money to get their hit. It worked as I thought it might, except I never had any equipment but like Dracula they all wanted my blood in the form of heroin. So, I was handed a tablespoon and a glass syringe and I was given some powder.

My eyes flashed across the room and like a computer, I took in everything, everything that the junkies were doing. So I ripped off my tie and wrapped it around my arm and my virgin vein was about to become one of the biggest slags going. I got a tablespoon, some water and a match and placed the powder onto the spoon. Then I lit the match on my jeans and held it under the spoon for several seconds, until it was in liquid form. After that, I drew the smack up into the syringe and I took a deep breath into my lungs and I don't fully remember what happened next for several seconds. How on earth can I explain the euphoria I see?

Euphoric.

(Flashback to the hospital.) I opened my eyes and blackness was all that I could see. I was totally blind. I went to wipe my forehead and I couldn't move. Not even my little finger. Then a blinding pain shook through the full length of my body. It was like no other pain I have ever had, a hundred times worse then a withdrawal symptom. I tried to call out for help and I couldn't speak and yet I could hear everything and comprehend. I was like a living corpse. I knew I was alive because I could think. That was when God must have intervened, because I had died for a period of 6 minutes!

I did a dodgy deal at the London Hilton Hotel. I had to get some information from a gangster so I took a briefcase which concealed a reel to reel tape recorder with a pen as the microphone! I arrived late to make the man feel like I was not too eager and I strolled in to meet him face to face. He was wearing a beige camel-hair coat with a Rolex and a diamond tie pin which I recognised more by the Jacques Faf tie. I could sum him up by these small details. I knew that he was a pro. I ordered a bottle of good whiskey with the intention of finding out what kind of

Richard Levesley

man I was dealing with. I poured him about a quarter full of scotch and this was another test to see if he was a drinker. The man said sharply "Fill it up!" and I observed him drink it quickly . . . I followed suit! Now this gave me a clearer idea of how rapidly I could question him. I began! I honed in on his watch and said

"Nice watch you have there," while pouring him another half of scotch. He didn't ask for the next drink. He took up the bottle and filled his glass full. I asked him how much he paid for his watch and he answered £275.

I replied "are you interested in jewelry?"

"Yes," he said. Right, now the business began.

"I might know where to get some gold,"

"What kind of gold?" he asked quizzically.

"The best 22carat,"

"Mmmmm. That sounds fairly good."

To an outsider that would sound as if he was not all that interested except to one who knew better . . . . now I had to watch and keep the whiskey flowing! I looked around and to my glee he drank three quarters straight down and I saw his eyes start to slightly glaze. I did not want him to get too drunk so I began my spiel.

"I might know some people who could get you what you asked for (gold)," and I carefully watched for his reaction. His pupils dilated . . . . great I thought to myself.

"How much are you talking about?" I said. There was a deathly silence which felt like an eternity, although it was probably a matter of seconds. "How much do you want and of what quality?"

"The best,"

"OK, let's talk business,"

At what price and how much, I thought to myself. It all depends on the next answer whether or not I have pulled it off!

Alright, I wanted a clear and loud answer for the tape. I spoke aloud . . . "Pardon?"

"Yes,"

I looked quizzically at his mouth and once again I got a clear and loud "YES" and I thought to myself "GOT YOU, you low life bastard! That's a wrap!"

At the age of six or seven my parents had just bought me a duffel coat and shoes. I was messing about in the square when I accidentally slipped and I went face down into a puddle. As I got up my new clothes were beyond recognition. I thought I couldn't let my parents see what I had done, so I decided to run away. My father had a tent so in a hurry I packed it into a shoulder bag and off I went. Not knowing where to go, BOX HILL was the only place I could think of because I had been there quite a few times. I hit Clapham Junction for a train, destination: BOX HILL. As I arrived there at around half two, I decided to climb the HILL face upwards instead of the normal way. It took three hours, at least, to reach the summit and it was getting cold. I was in such a hurry to leave my house that I was kinda not thinking rationally and I forgot to grab any food. So there I was on top of Everest without any oxygen or so it seemed. All I had was a bar of chocolate. It sure took it out of me, the climb. I was totally exhausted and cold and hungry. (Not for the last time in my life) Hastily, I started putting up the tent and low and behold, I was one pole short. By now I was getting colder and the climb kept flashing through my mind. What an achievement, I kept on telling myself because that hill had a 1/8 gradient. (It also had hidden pitfalls!)

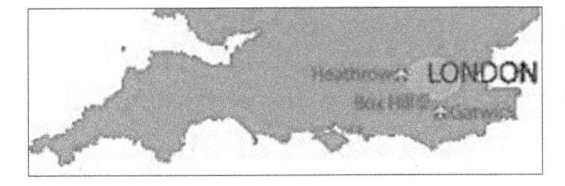

Now I had to look at my options, either freeze to death or starve. If my memory serves me well, I recalled a telephone box somewhere on the summit, so I took it into my own head that I had to find this elusive telephone box and fast. I gathered all my strength and, like a vision out of the bible, there it was, only a few steps away. So, I wanted to get into some kind of warmth. I had packed a Primus stove and I hastily set it up and, like a simple twist of fate, I'd forgotten the matches. I screamed out "AAAAAAAAHHHHHHH!!!!!" and there was only one thing left to do, dial 999.

"Which service do you require: fire, ambulance or police?"

I croaked out "Police," and I felt kinda wretched and defeated. Within half an hour or so they arrived, sirens blaring. They took me down to the station and I told them roughly what had happened and they didn't have any way of contacting my parents. So, before I got away from the clutches of the police, like a criminal, I asked if I could make a telephone call. At the back of the flats where my parents lived, there is a police station, so I made a call to them and this is what I said. I gave them my full name and address and asked the sergeant if he could knock on my door and say to my parents that I am stranded and have run away and I want to come home. There was no means of transport offered by the police. Fortunately, my father had a Ford Popular, so in the early hours of the morning my father set off to drive to an unknown destination: BOX HILL. Several hours later, I saw headlights appear on the horizon, with mixed feelings, not knowing what his reaction would be. But before I had too much time to reflect on what I had done I felt two strong arms hug me and all my troubles seemed to melt away like icicles.

Scruffy Pete and Andy were a couple of friends of mine, whom were frequent goers to the Two Eyes coffee bar, where we met and became like the three musketeers: Athos, Aramis and Porthos. Each of us had a talent. Pete's skill was in pick pocketing, Andy's was the charmer, and as for me, I had a combination of the two. So, I had an idea that we should all take a vacation, destination: MAJORCA. In the sixties, the island of MAJORCA was a mere speck on the map.

I knew that we were low on gear and cash. I had made enough money from the Hilton deal to score and get all of us out of England. Dover to Calais took my last penny, so it was up to me to think of something. Hitch-hike. I told the guys to hide and stood by the roadside. After a few minutes, a car whizzed by, so I am learning all the time. This time I was prepared. I used my hearing and my sight and first I heard a car approaching, worked out how long it would take for the car to reach me, which was within a matter of seconds. I wasn't going to let this car pass. I stepped out into the road and put my thumb up. The car screeched to a halt and I said to the driver "Are you going anywhere near Paris?". "Yes, in fact I am going all the way," and at that moment when he opened the door I gave the wink to my mates to get in the car quickly! Before the driver had time to think we were on our way.

Scruffy Pete had already dipped the bloke's wallet and Andy was chatting with the driver, while I was checking out the route on a map and in a sinister way, was watching Aramis and Porthos at work. Once we had reached our destination we all said our farewells and, with the upmost courtesy, we graciously stepped out of the car, right in the heart of Paris.

It was an unwritten law that all the takings were handed to me. Scruffy Pete had picked a fat wallet, so we all had a fix and full bellies and a luxurious place to sleep, except Pete didn't jack up, he was a pill popper. So, while Aramis and I slept Scruffy Pete was pacing the floor. When Athos and Aramis (me and Andy) woke up, Porthos (Scruffy Pete) was still pacing the floor and I was feeling very content. So, we went on a sight-seeing trip, believe it or not!

INTO MY VEINS

The Champs-Elysees took my breath away, and in the distance, low and behold, stood the Eiffel Tower. "I must get to the top," I thought to myself. As we approached the Tower it looked bigger and bigger. I had a rush of adrenaline running through my veins, as if I was expecting something phenomenal. Scruffy Pete was with me, so onwards and upwards! It took around five minutes to reach the top by lift. There are three stages to the Eiffel Tower. This is an important detail as it was our escape route. I am not afraid of heights but Scruffy Pete is. We stepped out at the top and Scruffy Pete had a hold of my arm and there was a souvenir shop. I looked around and I was amazed at the sights. The Arc de Triomphe looked aesthetic as I had read about it and the Champs-Elysees was a wonder to behold. It was very busy and there were many people, so that meant where there's people there is money. At first, I didn't notice that the till was a draw-till and all the assistants were putting in loose francs. I guided Scruffy Pete towards the till, expecting him to do his job, except he had lost his bottle. It was up to me to take control. Like grease lightning, I had opened the till and took both hands full of cash. Scruffy Pete was too scared to even move, let alone grab a fistful of francs. At the corner of my eye I clocked a gendarme and they don't mess about. They also carry guns. So, I knew that we had to get out and down and fast. I slung Pete over my shoulder and the lift was the only means to get out of the shop. So, the lift door opened after what seemed a long time and it was crowded. It went down except it was going so slowly that I had to think of an alternative method to get us down. So, when the lift stopped at the first stage, I saw some stairs and the time was slipping away. I had to make an executive decision, take the stairs at the second stage and now or run the risk of being caught. I took the first option and hit the stairs. The stairs were open air, with only a bar to hold on to. With Scruffy Pete still motionless over my shoulder I came close to death, as I ran three steps at a time. Like a rat following the pied piper, I was scurrying down the tower to the second stage. One false step and we would have both been killed and Pete wasn't getting any lighter. I was nearly out of breath and my

legs were turning to jelly. After the epic descent of 905 feet, with a final 177 feet to go, I did slip. Pete came round and stuck his foot out and I took the full force of us both. It prevented us once again from a massive injury or we cheated death.

Or so I thought, because I heard a loud French voice shout "HEY, ARRETEZ (STOP)." At that signal, my brain went into overdrive and we both fell the rest of the way, which fortunately was about thirty feet. At this point Lady Luck took a hand in what should have been enough to have either killed or fatally injured us. What prevented the fall was a mass of tangled arms and legs. I came off worse, with a cut on my forehead and I kinda liked the feeling of true blood running down the side of my face. Pete, however, didn't get away scott-free. He had several bruises on his arms and legs. So, we still weren't safe except we were on the ground! "ARRETEZ!" was getting louder, so that meant the gendarme were nearly on top of us. I don't know what it was except there was a taxi waiting there, as if it was meant to be there. I helped Pete to his feet and I yelled to the cab "Hang about, mate!" and once again we were on our way!

First, we had to get Andy, but as usual Andy had charmed his way and was in bed with some girl. I yelled to him to get his arse out of bed because I was feeling a mixture of emotions, which were fear, elation and desperation. Andy was quick to react to my voice because he was on my wavelength. The apartment was at the back of the Champs-Elysees. I threw some cash at the landlord and said: "Au Revoir!" At this time the taxi took us to the Gare du Nord Train Station. It was as if it was meant that we were guided onto the right train. I hadn't started to count the bounty yet, I was thinking more about our next move. At the back of my mind was to get as far away from Paris as possible. After a while I got bored sitting on the train, it wouldn't have been so bad if it was a freight train. I told the guys to jump out at the next stop. We weren't getting any richer and the gear was getting lower.

Once again we were on the road. Several cars stopped and we repeated the same method of gaining cash, except Pete was not able to do his job. Andy was unable to pick a wallet without getting caught, so I had to do the work of two until we got a ride most of the way. It was a Juggernaut. I kinda liked this way of travelling. So, we were almost at the French border when the geezer had to take another route. I did leave a few francs on the dashboard as gratitude.

It was not far from the border, so exercise and fresh air were called for. All of us hadn't done much walking, except for the occasional burst of speed. We got through the border on a temporary passport, except the German border was a different kettle of fish. For a start we had gear on all of us, in one form or another. The German border guards were like the SS, very thorough and meticulous. I was cool as ice, Andy was kinda worried which I could see by his demeanour and as for Scruffy Pete, I could see a bead of sweat appear on Pete's forehead. I did a one finger gesture across my forehead indicating to Pete that he had to stop the sweating and we may have a chance. To fool the 'SS' as we approached the Checkpoint, I took the guys to one side and like a coach briefing his players into action, I told them that if we blow this we're looking at 5 to 10, minimum. I checked their heart beats and Scruffy Pete's must have been going like the clappers. I had to wait until Scruffy Pete's heart was as normal as possible because he had taken several purple hearts which apparently increases your heart beat. So there was nothing I could do except give Scruffy Pete and Andy a firm talking to. With that they both calmed down. Right, now we are ready to face the formidable 'SS'.

With much trepidation we proceeded to be interrogated. I sent Scruffy Pete first because if he got through then I knew that Andy and I could make it through. After what seemed like an age, Scruffy Pete made a gesture with his outrageous scarf indicating that he had made it! It was Andy's persuasion and charm which got him through, his gesture was a fist. Now it was my turn. They took one look at me and I passed through without any cross words spoken.

Now, we are in what felt like an alien country, yet my senses told me that this was going to be a prosperous and lucrative land. After several hours into Germany I had remembered that in London I had met up with a Danish girl called Nadia. So now the aim was to get to Copenhagen.

Nothing really happened, except when we got to Hamburg. I went to the toilet and I felt itchy and I had been feeling itchy for quite some time. I glanced down and to my horror I saw something move: CRABS! Not knowing how they got there or how to get rid of them, I asked the others if they had the same symptoms. They answered 'No' which threw me into a rage, so I jacked up and went to the nearest bar. A bottle of gin was in order. The effect was kinda what I had in mind. It didn't help the crabs any but it sure helped me. A bloke came and spoke to me and asked me what the trouble was because I must have looked kinda desperate. Fortunately, he spoke immaculate English and I was in no state to worry about what gender he was. I didn't want to tell this stranger until I could feel a crab bite me, one of thousands. Then I poured all my woes out and to my surprise he seemed to know exactly what it was and how to cure me of this horrific plague!

I finished up the bottle and rolled up my trouser leg and lo and behold there was as many of them as there were needle marks on my arm! He took me to the green cross sign (a chemist). He spoke to the guy behind the counter in his mother tongue, and translated as he spoke each word. He asked for some liquid to cure crabs. It was a white cream with an applicator in the form of a wooden elongated spatula. I didn't know how to show how grateful I was. I began to put my hand in my hip pocket and as I did so he placed his hand on mine as if to show that money was not necessary. He took my hand and shook it firmly and we parted without another word spoken.

I felt humbled at his kindness. After that heavenly gesture I was brought down to earth with a jolt by what felt like all of those alien creatures taking their revenge . . . they attacked my body as if they all took a bite at the same time. So I ran as fast as I could back to the others and took off my trousers, flinging them across the room. Without any hesitation I smeared the lotion on as if like a man obsessed. I sat on a stool and watched with amazement as the crabs dropped off like flies. All that was left was thousands of holes where they had been sucking my blood.

After this misdemeanour, which I rapidly put to the back of my mind, I took all of us for a tour of Hamburg and what a tour it turned out to be. I am not sure whether trouble follows me or I follow trouble because this turned out to be heavy trouble. We were casually walking down the street when I felt a hand touch my bum. I turned around sharply to see who it was and in an effeminate voice I heard "Are you English?" and all three of us said in unison "Yes." The person answered "fancy a coffee?" Without hesitation we all agreed on "Yes". I could see like a camera lens; photos flash through all of our heads; a place to crash and money. It wasn't long before we were already choosing where to sleep and sussed out how much he was worth. "Hmmmmmm," I thought to myself, "a pretty penny."

After a few days, I knew the layout of the apartment and I clocked a wall safe. So, I was in no hurry to leave. The temptation got the better of me. So, I cracked the safe with ease. I haven't had such a fright for a long time. Staring at me was a Colt .45 laying on top of an enormous amount of money. What to do next? Fingerprints were all I could think of. It was like a rattle snake ready to strike on a gold bar. So I knew the only thing to outwit the snake and that was to throw a rag on top of it, thereby blinding the snake and blinding me from the Colt. I took the money out with great care not to leave any prints. I closed the safe and wiped the dial and I left some Deutschmarks as a token. We left as casually, as casually we came.

Richard Levesley

I had heard of a red light district and the notorious night club called The Star. Scruffy Pete went to the red light; myself and Andy took to the club. We could get girls wherever and whenever we liked. Therefore the Star had an alluring attraction . . . . it satisfied all expectations. Once inside flashes of the Flamingo went through my mind. It had a similar ambience and lighting. I got talking to a chick that was quite tasty. She told me that I had not long missed the Beatles. I wasn't really into the Beatles at that time as my roots were blues. While she was telling me, I had one hand up her skirt and the other hand was dipping her bag. I left her in a state of ecstasy and remorse. Now, my eyes flashed across the club like a computer, searching for another victim. Andy was doing the same. I felt a presence behind me and a tap on the shoulder. My whole body turned to ice and I spun around with my flick-knife at the ready. I was expecting a polizei. To my astonishment, there stood Scruffy Pete, with his hair like a mashed up beehive and his outrageous scarf, looking like a scarecrow. I could have kissed him! He was excited to tell me of his exploits. I gently put my hand across his mouth to stop him speaking. I felt the blood run back into my body. Pete's wounds had got better and he was able to make up the working threesome, a force to be reckoned with. I could go on. The hour was getting late, so we said farewell to the club and the night. I threw back some Deutschemarks at the Star Club. It became my trademark. It was a sign of thanksgiving.

As usual, we had more money than gear and Hamburg was the place to get it. It didn't take long before we were handing over some of our ill gotten gains for H and Pete's tabs. Happy as Larry, once again! We were on the road. By my calculations, we were close to the Danish border. The journey was over quite quickly, we found the Germans to be extremely obliging and generous. I was so near and, yet, so far from the formidable Danish pass to my objective, which was to see Nadia. Again, I was taken by surprise and we waltzed straight through.

Flashback to Soho

In a coffee bar called 'Le Marcarb', the entire decor was coffin tops and skulls and very dark. All the other girls were quite plain, except one, who was wearing a fur hat. I honed in on her and introduced myself. It wasn't long before I had got all the necessary information; for example, she was Danish and lived in a small village and had a sister. I took Nadia to the cinema to see Lawrence of Arabia. I said to her "Excuse me, I have to go to the gents." The lights went out. I walked out into a sheet of pitch black and, for the life of me, she had disappeared, like a swamp had swallowed her up. I wanted to see the movie, so I sat through the whole film alone. When the lights came back on, to my amazement, I saw the fur hat. My heart skipped a beat and, lo and behold, there she stood. I took her to the nearest pub and ordered a double and a lager, presuming that she drank lagers.

After we had chilled I walked her home, not before I had got her full name and address.

DENMARK was a flat country, quite Hans Christian Andersen at first glance. It took several attempts to get a ride. Mind you, I'm not surprised because the Danes were rather pristine in their clothing and, to the Danes, us three looked like we had just stepped out of a horror film. Although we did eventually get a lift to our destination, which was a place called Odense. I wrapped on the door and there Nadia stood, just like it was in the cinema. She threw her arms around me and kissed me hard on the mouth. She pulled me inside and beckoned my friends into her house, which looked like a page from a magazine. We had arrived quite early in the morning, and for breakfast there was delight after delight! For example, an exotic aroma of coffee served in bowls and brown pumpernickel bread. After several days of doing nothing except making love and meatballs and countless bowls of coffee, I began to get bored. I decided to take the guys out for a bit of excitement!

In the village there were plenty of shops, so on the spur of the moment I told the guys that they can steal whatever they wanted, and I did my own thing. I stole 2 air guns and feeling generous I actually paid for the lead pellets, and took myself off to get some practice.

Meanwhile, Andy had got some black hair dye and as for Scruffy Pete, his contribution was three pairs of leather gloves. We took ourselves off and decided on what could we contrive with these items. In all innocence, I dyed my hair black, slipped my hands into the leather gloves and put the air guns into my belt. The next thing I knew, a pair of handcuffs was slapped on my wrists behind my back and before I could comprehend what had happened I was banged up in jail! Shortly after Pete and Andy were thrown in the cell with me. We all looked at each other in bewilderment, not knowing the whys and wherefores until it hit me what could be a reasonable explanation.

I had been making out with Nadia's sister (her name escapes me) piecing it together like a RICHARD DADD fairy fellows masterstroke jigsaw puzzle. I came to the conclusion that somehow my appearance, with my hair dyed black, a pair of black leather gloves and 2 guns in my belt, could have put a picture of me as a criminal into the minds of the two sisters. Whilst I was pondering over the situation the police came in and with a perfect English accent, told me that they had received a call from the Olsen sisters saying that they had some criminals under their roof. With that, the younger sister sent a guard into the prison cell to ask me if I would see her. I was so outraged that I declined the offer. I kept on saying "No," and each time he came to see me he tried to persuade me by saying that she was crying; which I understood to mean that the sisters were feeling remorseful. Then I knew that I was 'not guilty'. In total we had spent two weeks without even a whiff of gear and Scruffy Pete felt his withdrawal the worst. So it is quite understandable why I said "No," to the guard. All we wanted was to be free from the cell and free from the sisters and to kiss Denmark farewell. Which we did.

So, the air smelt good and clean now, after being cooped up for a precious two weeks in jail and two weeks of my life. Not knowing what the future had in store for me, two precious weeks was an awfully long time. The first thing we had to do was to score some H. Which I managed, with great difficulty because the Danes were a clean and healthy country. They weren't into drugs all that much.

We had to get our thumbs out for a ride. All was well and all went well. On the first ride, I took out the map to check where we were heading and, with one glance, I could have sworn under my breath that it would have to be double-back the same way as we arrived through Germany.

An incident happened that I got put in jail in Frankfurt. I must apologise that I cannot recall it.

According to the map, we had to go through France to reach my vision: MAJORCA. Nothing really happened this time. In fact, we sailed through Germany. Before I knew it, we were at the French border. It is always scary going through any border with gear on all three of us except if you know how to cope with the anxiety and pressure. Although, one can never expect or take the one-off chance of being caught. As usual, the expected became the unexpected and, before we knew it, the Eiffel Tower was in the distance. This time we gave it a wide berth!

The French people I took to straight away and their fashion was right up my street. In a French quarter called Montmartre, which was a mixture of bohemian and futuristic people, I spotted in a shop window a long, black, leather jacket, which I had to have. So, I did the same trick of putting two coats on and only giving back one. It was such a large object, that I had half up my sleeve and half down my trousers. I chose a brown one because I did not want any thoughts of what had happened in the past in Denmark, of looking sinister. And, man, did I look cool! I looked like Clint Eastwood in The Good, the Bad and the Ugly except I felt much cooler.

We plodded on through France with nothing to write home about and before I knew it the Spanish Border was a Tom Thumbs lift away.

As much as I hated crossing borders I had a premonition of crossing this border so I was prepared for any eventualities. Right here we go! I had heard that the Spanish Borders were thorough and extremely meticulous in their methods of searching. I watched from a distance to observe how and what their routine was and cor blimey, what a good job I did taking in how they did it. First they watched for any signs of perspiration and I did notice that on occasions they felt the beat of your heart. So I told Scruffy Pete to get rid of his purple hearts and he swallowed all of them. That gave me an idea . . . if I could put my stash, which was wrapped in Cellophane, in my mouth I could swallow if I chose to before I spoke. In fact, all our stash was getting low and by now I had changed from pills to powder, and yet it was still enough to kill me. So, we drew matches to decide whose fate it was to go first. Andy drew his match first and it was long and Scruffy Pete wasn't going to draw any, so in my anger I snatched at the last remaining two matches, I drew one out slowly and it was the short one. I should have made the others go first because, being the cool one, I could handle the situation better. I placed the stash in my mouth at the last moment and I got singled out. I was given a thorough body search, and they sure don't mess about. They placed a hand on my heart to check if my heart was racing. At first, it was going ten to the dozen, so, I switched everything off in my brain and it began to slow down. They held my passport up in front of me. I felt that they were trying a psychological approach and I had to get out of this situation fast because the cellophane was beginning to melt. I had one last option left. It would either kill or save me. I reached into my coat and pulled out several thousand francs and with a gesture I offered them what could have been a good bribe or the opposite. I saw them look at each other and said a quick prayer. Are you still with me, Lord? At first I thought I had blown it. I took another thousand out and slid it under the blotting paper with the rest and I watched their faces to see what the reaction would be. To my amazement they slipped the cash out and said "Vamos!" I couldn't see what was going on with Andy and Pete, except the lucky bastards came through with a smile that could have cracked a mirror. Scruffy Pete was as high as a kite and Andy had the foresight to jack all of his smack before he came through. I spat out the hoard that was almost killing me slowly. I wasn't too disappointed because I was getting a high and as for Pete, well his eyes were like saucers. Like I said before, me and Andy were on the same wavelength.

We humbly crawled into Spain, one foot at a time, without anything except one ambition—MAJORCA. We arrived in Madrid and I had noticed that my addiction was getting worse, a slight observation on my part. We made our way to the airport. We pooled all our cash together and got enough crumpled filthy money to purchase a ticket on an aeroplane. The airport was a cinch, except the aircraft was like the worst horror ride you could possibly imagine, as we found out once we had taken off. It was a horrifying ride. For one, the thing Andy hated was the fear of flying. Second, Scruffy Pete was sick and had diarrhoea. And as for me, I came off worst. Well, I thought so because I was perspiring and had severe stomach cramp. Anyway, we just about staggered out of the flying hell, not before I kicked the aircraft.

INTO MY VEINS

Once again, it was an easy exit through the airport, and it was like Neil Armstrong putting one foot on the moon, as I stepped out of the whats-it-called and put my foot on MAJORCAN SOIL!

My first thought was to get my sickness under control. It is amazing how junkies recognise each other so, it wasn't that difficult to score. We had forgotten one small detail: we had lots of cash except it was in the wrong currency. But I was in no position to mess about, so I paid double for a few grains of H. And I was in no fit state to worry about the other two. I rushed to the nearest bog, and took off my leather jacket, and I reached for the nearest thing for my arm, so I ripped off my belt as a tourniquet. I had begun to feel better already. It wasn't long before I felt normal once again.

just coming down

I took it upon myself to find Andy and Pete. I came across them both in a bar and they were trying to get stoned, as they hadn't scored. I took Andy back to the place where I met the guy who sold me some H, because I knew that where there is one there will be more of the same. So, although I couldn't find the guy, I found lots of dealers who would sell me a reasonable deal. Both of us got more than enough to last a while.

I started to get an abscess on my arm, so I went to a green cross chemist for something to take away the abscess. I showed the woman behind the counter my arm and all she could recommend was DDT (a strong disinfectant) which eventually did the trick. While I was in there I saw some Mandrix. Although they weren't purple hearts they had the same effect. So, I bought a couple of tubes with about a hundred in each and gave them to Pete to try. To my amazement, they didn't ask for a prescription. When I saw Pete's eyes like flying saucers I knew that Scruffy Pete is in his seventh heaven.

Now we were all set, I could relax and fulfill my vision. I decided to check out the beach and it was like finding Man Friday's footprints on virgin sand. The apartments overlooking the beach were as white and luxurious as if owned by millionaires. Right, I had to get in with this crowd. So, I lay on the beach with the most evocative position and was slowly stroking my six-foot frame with oil and waited for some honeybees. It wasn't long before I had my first bite.

It took the shape of a woman, quite elderly and I could tell by her skin that she was either a resident or had been there a long time, because it was unusually tanned. As it happened she was just on holiday, so I knew exactly what she wanted. Who was I to argue? So, off we went back to her hotel. I took a quick fix and it was quite an easy thing to satisfy her. She fell asleep in my arms and now I had to get her head and body lying gently on the pillow. I kissed her softly on her breasts to make sure she was fast asleep and, getting no response, I slipped out of her arms and laid her on the bed. I could not wait for her to reward me, so I took all of her cash and travellers cheques.

It was hot and humid, so I took a swim in the ocean to attempt to wash away my sins. I had a belief in God from quite an early age but that didn't stop me from committing all the crimes, although I wasn't aware of the fate that was waiting in store. Anyway, back on the beach, I took up a Raphaellian position and by this time, even though I thought it to myself, I was like a Greek God. Several hours went by and I was feeling a bit sleepy and the sun was beginning to set, so I went back to our bed and breakfast. Andy and Pete were crashed out, so I joined them and called it a day.

The following morning, as we had made friends with the local drunk, we all went to the bar for a lager or two and he was a brandy drinker. He had a portable radio and an empty bottle, and I had missed the sound of any kind of music. The options were obvious, so, handing over a couple of travellers cheques, I got a classy radio for next to nothing. This put my soul uplifted to hear some sweet tunes.

I took myself down to the beach. I didn't have anything in mind except to get bronzed and to listen to some music. So, I strategically placed my frame underneath millionaire's row and turned on to some tunes. I fell into a slumber for a couple of hours and I was awoken by a shadow, then I turned over onto my back only to see a man. We got talking and I told him where I was from and he was an American called Ray, who lived directly above my head, which happened to be one of the houses that I had mentioned earlier. Of course, I took up his offer of a drink and felt the cool marble floor under my feet. Everywhere I looked there was gold taps, door handles and a bar of solid gold and on the walls was Kandinski, Rembrandt, and to top it all, a Picasso. In the corner stood a Henry Moore sculpture. I was blown away because they were some of my favourite artists. The ceiling was made out of what I thought at first glance to be glass, except on closer examination it was a translucent material, which was a toughened plastic.

We talked into the small hours and I was always conscious of how much I was drinking. Apparently, he owned some stocks and shares as a side line, and the bulk of his millions were from inheritance and he owned a fleet of yachts. So, you could say he was worth a pretty penny! I gave him some of my opinions on art. Whilst we were talking he asked me if I would like to stay and I mentioned about Andy and S. Pete and I said that I would introduce them to him. So, like a streak of lightning, I was there and with Andy and Pete by my side. I didn't tell them what to expect.

So with anticipation we set off to meet Ray. As we approached 'Millionaires Row' I could hardly control my excitement. As we came closer to the white house I had to brief Andy and S. Pete that: "if you mess this up I will disown the pair of you." I told them that this man was a millionaire and lived in a pure, unadulterated, luxurious villa. I casually knocked on the what I felt was an 18 carat gold door handle, and was greeted with a silver-grey haired forty year old man, who was wearing white trousers and a blue and white checked shirt with sleeves rolled three quarters up his arms; extremely sharp and smart. I introduced Andy and S. Pete to Ray and watched for his expression. A warm smile greeted us. He beckoned us in and I saw Andy's knees buckle under him, and as for S. Pete, his eyes went as big as if he had walked into Aladdin's cave.

Ray asked each of us what we would like to drink. I took this as a character reference. I asked Ray for a tomato juice and Andy asked for a scotch, and so did Pete. I gave the boys a look of distain, they knew exactly what I meant and from the next round they had soft drinks. We talked most of the day about all sorts of things and I gave the boys the wink to go. I was interested in what Ray's opinion was going to be on what he thought of my friends because I wanted to stay in this wonderful villa with Andy and Pete. I asked him outright and to my delight he said: "Yes!". I asked Ray whether he liked Andy and Pete because I wasn't sure about all three of us staying and, to my astonishment, Ray replied: "I have got all of this house and no-one who appreciates it, like you do." I went outside to tell the boys that they had done well and I'm pleased to announce that we can all stay.

Although Ray was gay he did not once ask or imply that he wanted sex with any of us. All he asked for was good company and conversation, which we gave to Ray in abundance.

In our long conversation we had told Ray that we all had various addictions, which he didn't object to as long as I didn't jack up in front of him. After about a month we were sitting in a bar, when over the radio came the announcement that Kennedy had been shot and from that night everything we were doing backfired. It took the life out of Ray because he was an American and life with Ray went gradually downhill. This carried on for about two months until we stole from a shop.

Richard Levesley

I picked out an electric razor and I was getting careless. Andy picked out some aftershave and Scruffy Pete picked out some scuba equipment. All three of us were caught outside of what seemed like an easy getaway. As we walked along the promenade a car screeched to a halt and out jumped three plain-clothed policemen. We were so nonchalant about getting away we weren't expecting anything, so, not a moment to react. They bundled us into the car. We were driven to the police station; they split us up so that we could not correspond with each other. They asked me if I had stolen anything else and of course I said: "No!", not knowing what Andy and Pete had been up to. After several hours I was handcuffed with my arms behind my back and was whisked off to a maximum security prison. I caught a glimpse of the outside walls; they were high with countless rows of barbed wire. There were three heavy doors, and each door had it's own combination lock, so that only the Governor knew how to open them.

I was pushed onto a dirt floor; as the dust cleared I began to focus. There were armed guards all along the top of the walls and the inmates were about 70 of all colours and sizes. They mostly had shaven heads and were stripped to the waist, some were standing and the majority were kneeling and I could tell immediately that these were 'lifers'. I felt petrified because I felt alone.

It was an open air jail and the sun was beating down relentlessly and I began to sweat. In the corner of the yard stood a bloke who obviously ran the black market. He towered at least a foot over me and was covered from head to toe in tattoos. He was wearing a shirt and had muscles that could knock spots off Schwarzenegger and the significance of the shirt was that he could afford to wear one.

I was wondering about Andy and Pete and, at that moment I set my eyes on Scruffy Pete, shortly followed by Andy. The elation of us being united was astronomical because I don't think for one minute I could survive in this hellhole without a friend. Once I had sussed out what our next move would be I got down to work.

I knew that it was not going to be easy for one. Fortunately, we had left all of our stash back at Ray's or else they might have thrown away the key. Although no one knew how long we had to stay banged up it sure would have been better than a lifetime because that is what we would have got if there was even a whiff of drugs. So I thought that we had better get the withdrawal over with first. The sleeping arrangements were a single piece of wood, about five feet apart and twenty to a dorm and no piss bucket. So, us three had it really bad because one drawback is that we couldn't be sick or mess ourselves, which was virtually impossible. I had a word with the bloke in the yard, who dealt out things for things and I managed to get some plastic bags for each of us. Although we were searched by guards going into the dormitory, I managed to conceal them with great difficulty, but enough to fool the guards. So, at least we had somewhere to throw up. It cost me a pair of socks, which was a good investment.

After about a month we slowly got the addiction symptoms under control. Once that was over I began to make some deals of my own. All of us came fully dressed in the latest designer clothes which I put up as our collateral.

I set up doing my own stall which was one big mistake. It started well until I felt an arm wrap around my neck and was lifted up off the floor. I knew right away who it was because of the tattoos. I was carried like this until we reached the dormitory and I was slowly being strangled. I was flipped upside down and was dropped within a few inches off the floor. This went on until I screamed. I've felt fear before but nothing like this. I was completely disorientated. He spoke to me and said two words: "Keep away!" I knew exactly what he meant. After regaining consciousness I had to tell Andy and Pete to clear the stall. I never spoke a word to anyone for fear of reprisal.

The food was soup, which might just as well have been dishwater, and a biscuit, which was supposed to have been bread except after one had scraped away the mould and the maggots first, served everyday, week in and week out. So, the food was the upmost important thing. I went back to the bloke who dealt me that punishment and I sold him a vest in return for bread rolls with butter. This went on until I was left with only a pair of jeans. Andy would have sold everything except his briefs and Scruffy Pete, I think, did! As time went by, I made one desperate effort for someone to come from the British embassy to visit me, The bloke with the tattoos said he could not promise me anything except he would do his best and I had noticed that he had his eye on my belt. So, I was kinda reluctant to hand over my belt, although I had no choice. Within a matter of hours, I was called to the governor's office. I had spent six months in that hellhole and, without a further word, I was released. I mentioned my two friends and they too were released. It was the geezer with the tattoos that got us out.

The arrangement was exile from Majorca and to pay the cost of the shipment. I agreed without any hesitation. The only problem was how to get six hundred pesetas without stealing it. Then I remembered the radio! It was easy to sell a portable radio in the early sixties as they were like an iPod of today. I took myself down to the square which was a meeting place for the locals and I had learnt to pitch from the tattooed bloke, whom I owed so much. After a short time I had offers ranging from three hundred to eight hundred pesetas and I managed to squeeze another fifty, which I quickly snapped up. So, I was in favour with the Gods! As fast as my legs would carry me I went to the embassy and slapped down six hundred on the table.

The next thing I knew, all three of us were sailing back home and as each wave hit the bow I felt a sense of comfort. I was clean and the waves took on a different perspective I had never seen before which clarified me and the sea sprays smelt like fresh cut grass. It took what seemed a lifetime to reach British shores and a quick stop at the exchange to get some English money. In those days the exchange was phenomenal.

The first thing was to get a cab into London and to pay a visit to my Ma and Pa. My Mother wept with joy to see me because I had been sending postcards from each and every country and a handshake from my Father which almost brought me to tears.

It was not long before I had a yearning to hit the town. It was my first day out when out of the corner of my eye I caught sight of a mini. It had four of the gangsters inside and one of them was David Littvinof and I knew what this meant. So, I spun around into the nearest shop which was a cobblers and, to my horror, it was closed. Littvinof was looking the other way. I had a matter of seconds to hide. Fortunately, the shop next door was a chemist and was open. My heart was pounding as if it was going to explode. I had to stay in the chemist for several minutes. So,

I asked the man if I could have a glass of water, which I sipped very slowly. As I was just about to walk out of the chemists, the mini slowly passed. I ought to have known what he would have done. I fell to the floor on my knees in the chemist, as I saw the car pass by. That was one of several escapes I had to come.

It was a flip of a coin that decided my fate because Littvinof wanted a toy boy, and a handsome young male, I suited all the catagories. I was always wary of the legend that followed David Littvinof and from that day forward my lifestyle changed from one thing to another. I was wined and dined and I was taken to visit all the so called famous people. I remember one incident that I was a frequent visitor to Jagger's house where famous people often frequented, and that I could go there alone. I was asked by Mick if I could score some coke, so I scored him a £5 bag. He took a taste and said: "Thanks, man!" I stood there waiting for my fiver back and I could feel my rage inside. So, with one punch I whacked him on the side of his head. I felt a tooth fly out of his mouth and he crumpled to the floor. I walked out of the door and gave him one last look, over my shoulder and out of his life. This was the beginning of Littvinof's influence on me.

I always had cash in my pocket which I bought suits with and handmade shirts and handmade shoes. So, life was kinda cool except one is never satisfied. David and I went flat-hunting and we tried several. There was one along the Victoria Embankment called The White Swan which would have suited me down to the ground, except I could tell by Litz' face that it was not up to his expectations. So, with a shove with his arm we were out of that area and heading towards Knightsbridge. Litz chose the ideal flat. The entrance was set back out from the high street and had a lift which took us directly into the flat. It was lavishly decorated and, for a city boy, the flat was breathtaking.

Littvinof—Don't be fooled by the bike

David was shaving when he called me and said: "I always use a cutthroat razor." Before I could even blink he had me in a strangle hold and held the razor to the side of my face and he said: "If you ever betray me I will make your face look like a mine!"

Now everything was so cool that it had to end and this is how it did. David Littvinof hid huge amounts of money and I wasn't supposed to know where it was, let alone touch it. Anyway, I couldn't resist the temptation. It was stashed in the grill of an oven which I thought was a good place to hide anything. I opened the top compartment of the oven and saw what appeared to be at least two hundred pounds. I took the first hundred and, to my horror, there was a German Luger. This was similar to the safe in Hamburg, except this gun belonged to someone who would use it. So, what to do? I did not want my head blown off so I took two ton and I slipped the gun into my belt. I took one last look around the flat, then took the elevator down. I knew that if I got caught I would surely have been killed. I was coming out of the flat when I walked straight into David Littvinof.

I knew that he was aware that I had taken the cash and gun but he did not let on. He said: "It is time to move," and Litz chose a basement flat in Kensington Gardens. I had a feeling that this basement was going to be my final resting place. It had a peculiar smell; one of dampness and one of death. As we walked into the House of Horror he punched me in between my shoulder blades, which sent me spinning across the room. This was not meant to knock me out, it was a warning blow of things to come and come they did.

He stripped me naked, except for my briefs and he slapped me about for half an hour or so and this was to disorientate me. What happened next will stick with me for the rest of my life. He grabbed me by the scruff of my neck and took me into the room with nothing in it, except for a light bulb with a long cord. He threw me on the floor and went and got a wooden chair. He picked me up as if I was a piece of rag, sat me on the chair, smashed the light bulb and ripped off the cord and, with force, he tied my arms and feet behind the chair. He left me for two days and nights, so that I was completely weak. I had wet myself and I was thirsty. As I heard the keys in the door I felt kind of relieved and, yet, terrified. He walked straight up to me and gave me one punch on my chin, and threw water in my face, which made me semiconscious. He took out his cutthroat and held it across my mouth and said: "How would you like to look like me?", as he slid the blade across my mouth without actually cutting. Then after a few more slaps he took the blade and, piece by piece, started cutting my hair with the razor. I was vain and David Littvinof knew this flaw in me. It took several hours before he had finished. I felt him cut my bonds loose and I slumped to the floor and what happened next is beyond my comprehension. He got a bucket of ice and threw it on my body and shouted at me to get dressed.

"I am not finished with you yet!"

Now this threw me into a mind game of what is going to possibly happen next. Littvinof chose another flat in Chelsea and this is my last memory. I was given several barbiturates and a pure dose of heroin and the next thing I knew was a bead of sweat running down my face and an excruciating pain. I had died for six minutes and I was in a coma for six months.

It was within walking distance of the hospital and Littvinof knew this. He did wait around to make sure I was dead before he called an ambulance. I was blind and couldn't speak or move and could only scream with pain. Another reason why he wanted me dead was because most of the time I was with him he took me to visit people of the underworld, such as the Krays and people of higher ranks and influential contacts, and I kept a diary of all of these events. I was among the few people who knew where David got some of his wealth. In fact, he was a professional gangster.

I was told this information by several doctors: that I had died and was comatose for six months. I was told this by the CID: all that went on after I couldn't recall anything.

I was made a ward of court as word got out that I was alive. And yet, one of Littvinof's associates, whom I recognised, managed to get in, by pretending to be an orderly and he took lots of photographs of me. I couldn't talk. All I was doing was screaming.

So, I couldn't converse with anyone to tell the CID officer what went on.

As time went on and I reached the age of where I was no longer a ward of court, David Littvinof managed to worm his way in. He brought me all the things that he knew I liked. For example, a drawing of a figure by Annigoni, books like Marcel Proust and valium. This was only the beginning as I was introduced to some friends like Martin Sharp, Lucian Freud and Robert Fraser.

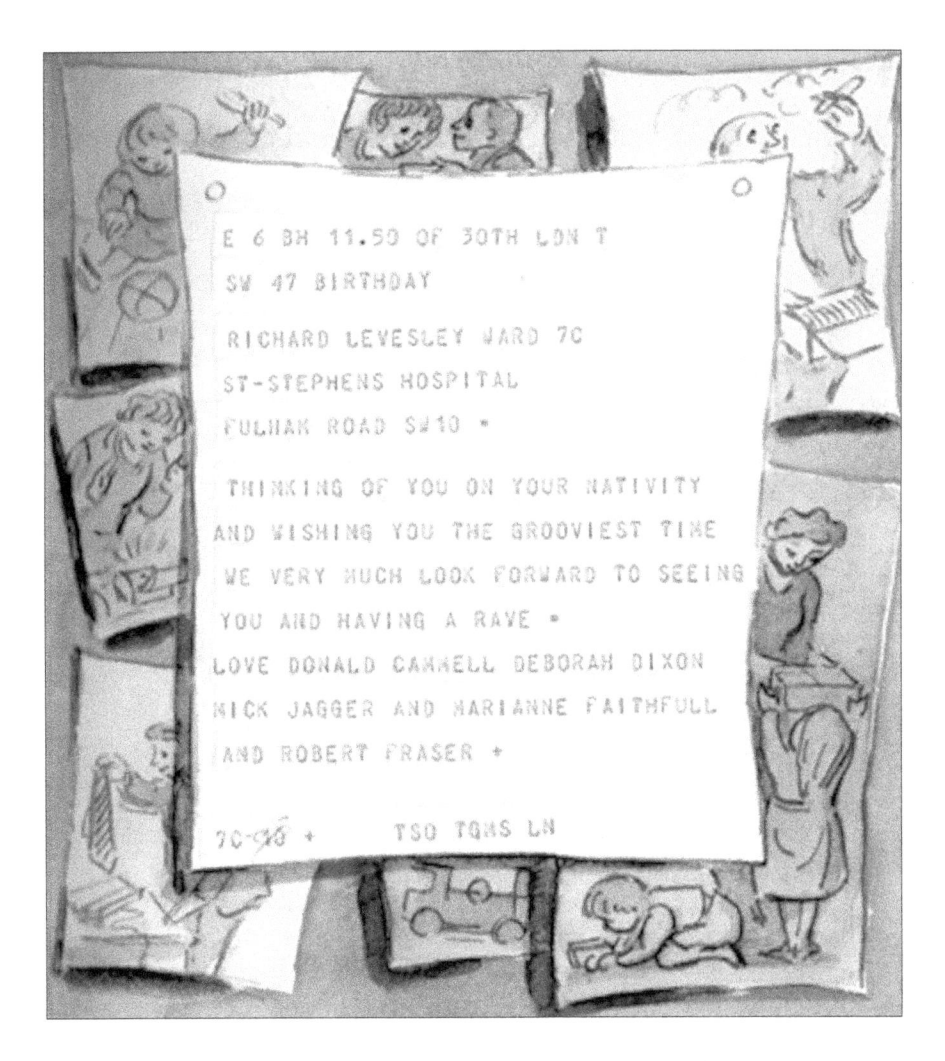

Get well card sent to me by Littvinof and Co.

It was my heart, which had shrunk, that was making me scream. Electrodes in my brain had been damaged, which really messed me up. It affected my eyesight and my speech and my motability. And what topped it off was my memory; I couldn't remember a thing. It took some years before I got my eyesight back. It was a gradual process until my eyesight was twenty-twenty. Tiny pieces of memory slowly returned. I had an alphabet board that I could communicate with, which I was prolific at.

My first spoken word was when my father took out a fountain pen and held it up and said: "Do you know what this is, son?" I felt like a static shock in my head and I pronounced the word "PEN," clearly, as if I was talking naturally. Once again my father asked me "who won the fight?" and I answered "Frasier," as clear as daylight. And I couldn't speak or say another word for years. I asked my specialist what happened to make me say these two profound words and he said: "Somehow your electrodes have mended," I asked him if there would be any further fusion and he replied: "It's a miracle that you spoke anything and I cannot promise that there will be any further repairs."

Meanwhile, back in the hospital, I was allowed one official visitor and that was my girlfriend with news that I had a son. She would keep in contact with me and the last I heard was that she had returned to Jamaica. No further contact.

In total it took four years of hospitalisation before I was finally out of the Chelsea Hospital and while I was in the ward I had built muscles like a professional body builder. It had underlying benefits; I went from a thin, withdrawn, Auschwitz-looking person to a Hitler-looking youth because my hair had changed colour to golden locks.

From Chelsea to Ealing in one foul swoop; to a place called Servite House. It was run by nuns and there were around twenty severely handicapped people and I had very little in common with any of them. I got on with the people who took care of me much better. In fact, I had a blowjob from one of the staff!

From Ealing I was sent to an old people's home in Richmond. I am not sure whether the nuns had anything to do with the misdemeanour because it was without warning and so quick a move. I questioned myself if that could be the reason. Well, anyway, I will never know.

I had a flare for art and whilst I was in Servite House I befriended the art teacher. She used to come with a bottle of red wine and help me mix the paint and she took me to her house, which gave me a sense of normality.

Talking of normality, Robert Fraser came to visit me. Now, Robert was a modernist and created furniture and he was well known in the art world. He was a smack head and Robert took me to his flat, which overlooked Saint James' Park. This will give you some idea of what his flat was like. There were three other people in the flat and Robert sacrificed his tablespoon of H and he gave it to one of the people who, in turn, gave it to me. I don't know why except it was given to me by mouth and I was sitting in one of Fraser's suede, futuristic chairs. I tried to hold it except I was pissing myself. I am not sure whether it was the drug or the drinks that we consumed in the pubs that filled my bladder but piss I did. I must have totally ruined a piece of Robert's priceless one of a kind furniture. Robert is normally a placid type but on this occasion he went berserk, shouting and swearing at me. The other people lifted me down and out of the flat and put me in a taxi. They told the cab driver that I was drunk and there would be someone at the old folks home in Richmond who would be there to take care of me. Eventually, Robert forgave me.

Robert used to take me out in a Citroen of the old style model car to see Christopher Gibbs at the Priory. The Priory was a magnificent building with acres of land and a gardener to look after it. It was such a beautiful place where Benedictine monks once lived. I was taken there often by various people including David Littvinof, who thought he had my friendship. So, it became a frequent meeting. Littvinof was an intellectual and extremely fluent in conversing and this is how he got on so well with Christopher Gibbs. Littvinof used to look after the Priory while Christopher was away on business. Therefore, allowing Litz to have the run of the abbey.

David Littvinof and Vivian Westwood

Only after many years later pieces of memory came flooding back. For example, I was told by the CID officer that I had a vest and y-fronts I was wearing when they found me and if I could have told the officer that I never wore vests and certainly not Y-fronts it would have helped my case against Littvinof. My parents took D. Littvinof to court and I could have had the finest barrister in the land except my mother wouldn't let my diary out of her possession. So, I was given a barrister who knew nothing about my case because the key to the downfall of Litz was in my diary. I think that my mother held on to it because she thought that I would definitely have been killed if she had handed it over. And the names and dates and businesses would have surely shopped a world of criminals.

So, David Littvinof walked out a free man except as the saying goes: 'What goes around, comes around.'

Meanwhile, in the Priory, Christopher took a month out on business, leaving D. L., once again, in charge. He had bouts of depression and it manifested itself in violent rage, which I had found out, to my horror. He took his rage out on me to such an extent, that I had to leave after several weeks. Gerry Goldstein was a friend of mine since the period of Andy and Scruffy Pete and we all met up at the Discotheque. I had quite a few good friends who frequented the club. Gerry arrived on the scene about the same time as Littvinof except he took a different route in the life of me. In fact, we went our separate ways. For example, he got married to some local loser. Gerry was quite an entrepreneur and he was into buying and selling books. I must admit that Gerry was my shadow from the time I first met him and still is.

My shadow, Gerry Goldstein

Gerry was with me at the Priory because I was a cripple and he pushed me around in my wheelchair and we both felt the full force of Littvinof's outburst, not for the first time.

Several weeks later, David Littvinof took his own life with a barbiturate overdose.

His body wasn't discovered for a period of nine days.

The gardener must have smelt the decomposing odor of the body.

In my opinion, Littvinof was crooked to the end because Christopher was expecting to see his so-called friend alive, after returning home from business. How I knew about David Littvinof's death was I heard it through the grapevine, except this wasn't an ordinary grapevine. It was almost mouth to mouth.

COLLAGE

THE SWIMMER

I stood on the Embankment with the River Thames in front of me. It was high tide and there were undercurrents I could see. So, I took off all of my clothes and in my mind this would prove to myself whether or not I was capable of a challenge. I took as much air into my lungs as I could and dived in. I was swept under by a powerful undercurrent and it must have been several minutes before I could surface. I took a gasp of air and I was always a good swimmer. So, I swam across and I got out at the other side. I looked across the River and I thought to myself "God, what an achievement! And I have got to do the return journey!" I was extremely fit, yet, I was thoroughly exhausted. I had to get back to collect my clothes. So, I dived into what I expected to be a perilous journey back. The journey back was just as treacherous but I had conquered my fears and got dressed as quickly as I could. My mates cheered me.

E-TYPE

I went into a car sales showroom and asked if I could take it for a spin. It was an E-Type Jaguar, black in colour and it was a convertible. I drove it along the Kings Road, past the Pheasantry where Annigoni and Timothy Widbourn once lived, and could have chosen one of a hundred girls, which I did.

I drove that beautiful car out into the country and I felt the wind hit my face as I passed the 120 mph and the girl, whom I shall not name, her hair was blowing in the wind. I kept on motoring until the petrol ran out, so the beautiful car had to be left by the roadside.

THE PHEASANTRY

I was fortunate to have stayed at The Pheasantry with Timothy Widbourn and Annagoni. Annagoni was painting the Queen and there were lots of freehand sketches everywhere. The studio catered for several people, of which I was one. The Pheasantry was like the Tardis and there were hundreds of rooms and studios with artists and photographers staying there.

The Pheasantry

VICTORIA STATION TO VICTORIA COACH

When I was a youngster I was always looking for ways of making money quite enterprisingly. So, I came up with the idea of carrying suitcases. I chose Victoria Station because it was always so busy and I had noticed that people were struggling to carry their suitcases.

I chose women mainly because of their weaker sex. My first customer was a lady who was trying to carry a whole lot of cases. I approached her and asked her if she would like me to help her carry her suitcases to wherever she was heading. Her destination was Victoria Coach Station, which was about half a mile away. Her reply was "Yes, please. I would be most grateful if you could carry my cases." There were two large cases. I lifted both cases with great ease and walked on, by her side. This took about half an hour to reach the coach station. As I'd hoped, she gave me a tip of 2/6 pence (12.5p). The next person was a bloke who was carrying three cases. I repeated what I had said to the woman and got the same reply. I put one case under my arm and one in each hand and this time the cases were HEAVY! I struggled back to the Station and was given a massive five bob. That would bring the total up to 7/6 (37.5p).

This went on until I had arms like an orangutan. In other words, until I'd had enough.

FEARLESS

When I was three-ish I lived at the top of a block of high-rise flats and I crawled out of the window onto a ledge. I was crawling along quite happily on a foot-wide ledge, not knowing that behind me was my mum going absolutely berserk.

Opposite was a neighbour, who was an old lady we fondly called the gorilla because she had a beard. She caught my mum's eye and was waving like a mad thing and she was pointing at me, trying to tell my mum that I was crawling along the ledge. At first, my mum just waved back until, eventually, she realised what was happening. I was oblivious to what was going on 'cos, although we were living on the top floor, it was just like a Sunday afternoon stroll to me. I had all the people out of their windows and doors. All screaming "Save him!"

A neighbour was the saviour of the day. My dad was at work at the time or else he would have done it. My neighbour could not crawl on a foot-wide ledge, so he tried to instruct me to crawl backwards. I did so, but it was incredibly difficult. So, he slowly inched his way towards me until he was balancing on top of me and scooped me up into his arms and that is how I was saved. He took me up in his arms and precariously inched me back safely. Cheers were echoed around the flats and once again fate took a guiding hand.

FIRE

I have got two sisters and myself and mother and father, on this rare occasion, were altogether, sitting in the front room on an autumnal evening. Mother was knitting. Father was reading the newspaper. I was busy with my stamp collection. Valerie was reading a book. Marion was on fire.

She had caught her nightgown on one of three bars of an electric heater. I was frozen to the spot, Valerie was in shock, Mother couldn't move and, like a flash, Father pulled the carpet with one almighty heave and wrapped it around Marion, who was, by this time, a burning inferno. His hands and arms were blistering in front of our eyes and as for Marion, thanks to the quickness of Father's action, she was saved without so much as a burn. And she went out on a date to a dance (to all of our amazement) the very same evening.

CARDIFF

My mother caught tuberculosis when I was 8 years old and she had to go in to hospital. At the time, my father was working at Dagenham Motors. So, there wasn't anyone to take care of us. I was taken in by my aunt who lived in Wales and, as for Valerie, she was taken to another relative up north. Marion was the eldest so she could look after herself.

I was extremely happy there. My aunt had two children of her own and I fitted in quite nicely. I have a couple of memories that will remain with me forever. I was walking across a field when I decided to take a shortcut. It was a sunny day and all I had on was a pair of shorts. I was half way through the shortcut when I did a nosedive into two huge banks of stinging nettles and each movement I made I got stung until I was literally covered from head to toe. So, I ran home screaming and crying. My aunt knew exactly how to treat my ailment. She smothered me with camomile lotion and I began to feel better almost immediately. I was put to bed and that was the most painful event of my twelve month stay.

Another fond memory I have never forgotten was every Sunday going to church. I was too young at that age to really fully comprehend what was going on, except I had a warm feeling every time I went.

My mother's rehabilitation was successful so, I could go back home and Valerie met me at the same time at the flat. She said: "Hello Richard!" and I said: "What?". It took several sentences from each of us to realise that Valerie had picked up a Geordie accent and mine was Welsh.

This period of time took a whole year. I don't want to blame this spell of time away for what went on in later years. Although, it was about the time I broke into my friend's house to steal fireworks.

WORKS

After leaving school I hadn't gotten anything in my mind about what kind of work I would do. So, it was purely by accident that I was taking a stroll when I saw in a lighting shop window: 'apprentice wanted.' I got the job. It was quite a distance from home so my parents bought me a 50cc bike. The wage was £3.50 p/w. Some of the jobs were interesting and they varied from prefab housing, to the luxury of Eaton Square, to machines in factories and to clubs of the so-called upper class. After about six months they knew that I was a good enough candidate to further my education.

They sent me to South Thames College once a week. I took to it straight away as there were many lady students. So, I was in my element. I found the paperwork easy and so were the girls. At the shop I got friendly with a white South African called Douglas Smith and his father was a well-known photographer. So, his son had access to lots of show business people whom I was introduced to. This was in the early sixties when people like Helen Shapiro, Adam Faith, Brenda Lee, Billy Fury and Marty Wild, to name just a few, had top billing. I got along with them because they were party animals and so was I. How I got along with them so well was because I was into blues and they were interested in what I had to say.

I worked in a restaurant in Sloane Square. I was the dumbwaiter and my job was to take orders and shout them down to the chefs. That lasted for fourteen days because I was in a cubicle and the heat was tremendous and there was a rope which I had to pull up and down. Up for the food and down with dirty dishes. My hands were beginning to blister and I had always fancied myself as a waiter.

THE CARLTON CLUB

This is one of my more exclusive occupations. It was in a high-class part of London called St. James' Street. I was extremely fortunate to have a position in such an elegant club. The Carlton Club is strictly for members of the Government. I happened to know the person who had just got the sack and he threw a few names who worked in the Carlton my way and that is how I managed to apply.

It was not an easy interview. Many obscure questions were asked of me and I just got the OK by the skin of my teeth. I was to find out later why these questions were so important because there were many MPs who liked to discuss white and on occasion green papers. White paper is when a group of MPs are discussing a political subject and green is when it is passed through Government (basically).

I was a wine waiter. I waited at Michael Heseltine's table, who was in the throws of ending a white paper and as I was taking his order, I was entering, in shorthand, into my diary what the white paper was all about. I put many overheard conversations from various other important members into my diary. Why I did this, I don't fully understand. If any of it got leaked out all hell would have broken loose.

I grew to befriend several MPs like McMillan, Douglas Home, and I got to know what wine to go with each member and what to say and what not to say. I worked at the club for about 6 months before I got bored. So, I handed in my notice.

COATS

When I was being wined and dined I couldn't help but notice the cloakroom or in several places, lack of. So, when times got rough I took it upon myself to make an opportunity of coats.

I did this by going into restaurants, ones without cloakrooms. Fur coats were in demand and leather coats were in fashion. So, this is how I turned coats into cash. I would choose a high-class restaurant and order a coffee and hang my coat strategically next to an expensive-looking jacket. It was fur and leather coats that got the most money and they were the easiest to sell. I would sit so I could keep an eye on the cloaks. I would down my coffee and pay for it long in advance so I had a clear getaway. I would scan the restaurant for people who are about to get ready to leave and make my move, choosing the most desirable coat and either putting it over my arm or wearing it. I would then walk casually out and run like hell.

In Soho, there was a notorious market for buying and selling everything, from fruit and veg to gold, silver, bronze and coats.

One gets to know who and what are buyers and sellers. I quickly learnt who was who. So I chose the best buyers and took the wares to Spanish Tony, who gave me the highest bid. Fur went at an astonishing rate of £15 and leathers at a lower rate of £13 and I was expecting it to be the other way around. Lighters and watches and any objet d'art I could take to Tony and get a fair price and I was not the only one. All this went on at the notorious Soho market.

MANCHESTER
LARRY PARNES

Larry Parnes is an entrepreneur who specialised in discovering future pop stars and managing already famous pop stars. He lived in a penthouse in London and was also a procurer of young boys, of which I was one. Larry P. took a shine to me and gave me a new set of clothes and a Dunhill lighter because he wanted me to meet Billy Fury. I met Billy in the suite and shook hands. Anyway, he took an instant liking towards me and asked Larry Parnes if I could come to Manchester because there was a Six Five Special show that Billy was on. All three of us got an express train to Manchester.

The Grenada Studio was only a stone's throw away from the train station. I was fascinated to look around the workings of a

TV studio. I was absolutely astounded when I was outside of the TV studio and a couple of girls asked for my autograph because they asked me if I was the lead singer in a band called the Crickets. I said: "Yeah," and I signed my non de plume, which was 'Ricky Duval'. Meanwhile, back in the studio, it was all go for the SIX FIVE SPECIAL and it was Billy Fury's time to hit the stage. Lights and Cameras were focused on him and he sung a blistering 'Halfway to Paradise' and a follow-up with 'I'd Never Find Another You'.

This took us a couple of days to get all the takes correct. We stayed in the Manchester Hotel and what I was dreading was the sleeping arrangements. Where was I going to sleep? It was three of us in a bed. Fortunately, Billy and Larry were so exhausted that they fell asleep as soon as their heads hit the pillow. The following day, Larry asked me if I could write what was going through my mind on a piece of paper. Hardly a Bob Dylan but it went something like this:

Can you see

<u>Part</u> (1)

Can you see

    my mind working like a cuckoo clock

    as I plug my fingers into the electric point,

    and lick the blood of the child of my stomach,

    and stick my crushed head in the gas oven

    in the flat off Tottenham Court Road,

    and eat chips with pincers stolen

    from a dentist retired to Bermuda?

Can you see

    me peering through the lavatory keyhole,

    and pouring fuel over every Van Gogh I see,

    set them alight and laugh

    my way to the Old Bailey,

    and stagger blind drunk down Wardour St.

Can you see

    my monogram stamped on every policeman's forehead

    and my footprints stamped on every front door

    in Cheyne Walk, as I fall into the Thames

and kiss my reflection in big store windows,

and paint obscene words on debs' behinds

and writing "I love you" on the posters

for sexy underwear on the underground.

Can you see

me kicking the Establishment, against the pricks,

with my hob-nailed boots that I borrowed

courtesy of West End Central.

Part (2)

Can you see

me in bed with a girl who I shall not name,

eating marshmallows provided by the postman,

and throwing her underwear in the bathroom

along with her, who I leave for a year and a day

to look at herself and make sure nothing's gone wrong

Part (3)

Can you see

how beautiful she is in the dawn

body pressing through cheap nylon

heavy with sleep and love

and, groaning, turns over again

pressing hands into her hot groin

in the cool of the dawn.

I don't know what happened to my lyrics, whether or not anything came of it, except I hope they get used.

On the return journey there was no way that I would ever envy any form of fame because as we were setting off back to London, we had a motor waiting outside of the studio and what a performance. First there were literally hundreds of screaming girls and two bodyguards for each of us and it was only a few metres from the exit to the car. It was like the killing of Mussolini except everything was preplanned. The driver had the motor running and all the appropriate car doors were open. I had my shirt torn and Billy was so well protected that he got into the car first, untouched. Larry P. was the same. We took off like a streak of lightning. Except that was the theory because there were girls throwing themselves onto the bonnet just to get a glimpse of B. Fury.

Eventually we hit the motorway hard. On the way back we pulled in at a greasy cafe. There were truck drivers who couldn't care less who or what the fuss was about. There were one or two autograph hunters and the rest of the caf' were pushing and shoving to get near us. Anyway, we managed to have a cup of tea and a few mouthfuls of egg and bacon. And on the road again.

MODELING

I fancied the idea of doing something with my good looks, so I found an agent who told me to get a portfolio.

That's how I broke into modeling. It was a successful enterprise and I did lots of catalogue work and a full length poster of me wearing a suit which was hung on walls in Knightsbridge, Soho, Earls Court and many more places. I was also an acquaintance of Michael McGrath.

Relaxing with a Jay

Mike had a stylish apartment with a unique feature: a two-way mirror hidden in the door panels and a sofa positioned so that the maximum view was obtainable. He was obviously a voyeur. It was close to Battersea Park, which in the sixties was an exclusive part of London. Going back to Mike's, he was gay and he had the mirrors especially fitted in the door panels. I took girls back to his apartment and it worked both ways for Mike and me. On my part, I had a plush place to take chicks for sex and as for Mike, only God knows what he got up to behind the door.

HOSPITAL TRICKS

I was first admitted into a twenty-eight bed ward but when I came out of my coma I was screaming so loudly that it disturbed all the rest of the patients. This went on for weeks, until I got put into a private ward. After several years, my screaming ceased and from then onwards, this is where I built my muscles (which I mentioned earlier) to a Herculean standard. Due to a flexing of muscles and tremendous spasms and contractions, it was like working as a bodybuilder for six years and I had never looked so fit and good. I put this into use because there were male nurses as well as female.

I have always been a highly sexual being, which had it's drawbacks and pluses. On the plus side I could get by on my physique and a handsome face that would get me all the things I wanted. And on the downside it would attract all the wrong sort of people. On one occasion, it happened to be a male nurse who gave me a shot of Physeptone. I had made acquaintances with some of the male nurses and I would go back to their flats and I could not inject myself, so, I had someone who could do it for me. And I also had many female nurses who admired my frame. I would sometimes ask to use the urine bottle and on several occasions, they would masturbate me into the bottle. I also got privileges, such as extra food and for desert, I could take my choice.

WINDOW DRESSING

I had a lover who loved me. She was older than I. We did everything together and her profession was window dressing. I used to do some work with her and I still think of her from time to time. Her name was Anne Headly-Johnson. When she went to work I used to go with her and help her create a classic window design and I remember doing a Harrods window with minimalist features. She had an office somewhere in the West End. I used to do lots of business, like, for example, I would go round various shops and with a business card, I would try to persuade the shop owners if they wanted their window dressed in a futuristic style. Some would say yes and some would decline. My relationship with Anne HJ was getting me down, so we started to argue and at this, I called it a day.

BLACK BALL

I had a friend called Michael Cleveland, who lived in a pub called The Red Lion. He was the son of a publican, whom I envied because he could get me cigars and cigarettes and shots of anything I wanted, such as whiskey, cognac and vodka, to name but a few.

One night we went to the cinema and I earned 1/6d and I don't want to tell any lies except just this one. I did a misdemeanour in the gents toilet and I am afraid you readers will have to use your own imagination. Earlier we had agreed that after we would go to the local snooker hall and Mick refused pointblank to go. So, in anger I threw the 1/6d at him and called him a few swearwords. That was the end of our friendship. I picked the money up and went on to the Snooker hall by myself. This was the beginning of another hidden talent.

This was the first time I had ever played.

I was a natural but I could still be beaten. I used to play for table games and there was a choice of tables. One of the cloths was far superior and the rest of the tables were worn and bold. I started on many of the older tables and quickly progressed to the two better tables. My maximum on the old tables was no more than 20 and on the better tables my score rate improved greatly. I think it shot up to about 98 and I took every opportunity to play.

It is like a game of chess and I moved from one snooker hall to another. Each time I played in better halls my game improved drastically, and my score rate shot up and up to 142. Now was the time to get noticed. So, I played for position to get my name called around the halls. I went from Wandsworth to Chelsea learning all the time. I started to play other players who had ranked the highest and amazingly enough, I beat them. I finally beat the best and that was the end of this little chapter.

TOOTH EXTRACTION

When I was in hospital I had a toothache which got an abscess. So, I was taken out of the hospital because they did not have the facilities to make any extractions. I was taken to a different hospital and I was placed in a ward with about nine other patients. They examined my teeth and made the correct diagnosis. When it came to my turn I was given an injection that put me to sleep and when I awoke I could not feel anything, because my mouth was still numb. The man opposite went down next and by the time he got back, I ran my tongue around my mouth and to my horror I had, what felt like, all of my teeth had been taken out. I couldn't speak, I still was using my word-board. I was told by the doctor that they had mixed up my chart with the patient opposite and I had twenty-two good teeth taken out. I was to find out later that the patient opposite had only had one tooth out with an abscess. (Now how ironic is that)

I guess I could have sued the hospital for mismanagement except my parents were of working class and were frightened by authority.

So the hospital establishment has got away 'scott free' from a law suit which would have cost them tens of thousands of pounds. The higher authority wins again.

DESIGN

Whilst in Servite House, they had various degrees of recreation. I chose art because I had been to art school. My motability skills weren't too bad and I had done some of the best artwork since I had my illness.

I even designed the disabled logo which today is world-wide. Of course, I had no idea that such a simple design would have created such a phenomenon. I painted it on a single sheet of grey paper with black water-colour and not even the art teacher recognised its potential. It was an exact replica of the standard issue that is recorded today. If only I knew then, what I know now.

That is the story of my life.

It's amazing what I've done on this planet in such a short time.

Richard Levesley

Milton Keynes UK
Ingram Content Group UK Ltd.
UKHW041303090824
1219UKWH00052B/382